The 1 Shame

A collection of my favourite poems

Shaine Singer

The Book of Shaine

published in Great Britain by

18 Yeend Close
West Molesey,
Surrey KT8 2NY

ISBN: 978-0-9576242-6-9

With thanks to Carly Longmire
"Vimy"

www.GJBpublishing.co.uk
@GJBpublishing

For Matt

I would like to dedicate this book of poetry to a great friend who believed in me always, which I didn't know, who suddenly died, a great friend and his family and friends have always been awesome and helpful.

Here's to you Matt

Matt, a bundle of joy, magic for life, a little strife.

The things you did and got up to, oh fantastic, oh true,

Adventure, the humour that added through drama,

Adrenaline, through zest of anything extreme.

But was a happy karma person that shines light, whoever knew.

Matt had faith in us all, he was super cool, music man,

With a love of horror, or true life stories, comedies, Star Wars.

I was the guess which film research and charismatic personality

Who knew luck, laughter through tears.

Matt is truly remembered always in our hearts and minds, he was also kind.

So here's to you Matt. Thanks for being there for a friend you can depend,

And all other friends who have known you.

What will you be doing up there?

Causing chaos and laughter, music,

So bright, loud and proud.

Thank you.

Contents

Shaine Singer

Shaine shot to fame as one of the stars of Channel 4's The Undateables.

This charming, gentleman poet became renowned for his love poems and won the hearts of many a lady.

Having grown up with a learning disability, Shaine had quite a sad childhood as he was bullied, but he found an escape through a love of poetry, drama and Doctor Who which helped him through these tough times.

Shaine's favourite poets include the likes of William Shakespeare, John Keats, Alfred Lord Tennyson, Spike Milligan and Pam Ayres.

Valentine Chocolate Heart

What am I?

Am I cuddly?

Am I fond?

Am I sweet?

Am I somebody's treat?

I'm passionate, elegant, radiant.

Better not melt.

It's a chocolate valentines heart.

From me to you.

Pier To Pier

Bournemouth shine,

Has a shrine,

Where surfers embrace the bluey green sea,

So much enchantment to see.

Bournemouth pier, so calm, quaint,

Then roaring waves hit the top of the pier.

Cold, whispers in the midst.

Pier so fair, so damp and less breath of air.

People walking on the pier, enjoying ice creams,

Fish and chips - inspires, or hotdogs, tea and coffee,

All the ones with mouth watering desires.

Boscombe pier, is dainty, glooming, dusky, quaint,

So pale shoulder of love reigns.

Has a fair bliss timeless quality, endless company

Or a picnic for two, serenading a love sonnet.

Pier to pier, we discover, uncover, the wonderous old fashioned piers,

That still test the time of long ago.

Bournemouth and Boscombe will always show passion, love.

Poetry writing will let the fun and pen flow.

Written In The Stars

Written in the stars,

People go far,

Near or like dust, or vanished without a trace,

Then dangers are in enemies paces.

Then something weird with a whooshing,

Wheezing sound of something comes.

A hit sci-fi series broadcasted in 1963,

On a cold dismal dark November night,

The day before, sadness struck and shocked the world,

The death of president JFK.

A Timelord who escaped his race, (Timelords)

The Doctor, 900 years old or more,

Stole a type 40 Tardis, and ended in 76 Totters Lane, London,

From Gallifrey, sounds like Ireland.

There's been many faces, many companions come and go,

And loads of enemies and villains have been beaten.

The legacy of the doctor has been carrying on as always.

And now comes the 50th special to come.

And also dawn of the 12th Doctor will rise,

And commeth the 11th will fall.

Regenerations, here we go again.

Who will it be then?

Relaxing

When you're feeling down, what do you do?
Have a nice cup of tea, cake or a poem
And maybe art or illustrations of passion, words, pure absolution.
But I read a book of poetry or a doctor who novel,
Or audio, to think of another dimension
Or unwind with a glass of wine or two,
Or watch a Doctor Who DVD with some Jelly Babies or mint humbugs.
Relax, we all need to do that, after a mad day
Or a weird one of zany week.
Unwind in places to visit, or have a adventure,
Full of humour, and passion, no drama or trauma,
But happiness and bliss.

Reality Is An Atmosphere

Reality is the fabric of the universe,
Little particles surround us all,
Out of the ordinary world, but out of the unknown,
It's a wondrous zone.
Is reality nice or stern or dangerous?
Can it be spontaneous or divinely outrageous?
We in distant times, slip away and back again,
From a weird and weary year, from now and then.
Can time itself be re-written, and start a new leaf?
Or a new chapter, or a new beginning,
Or a wonderful ease of a chapter one?
Life is strange, like a planet we see,
We watch, we deliver, we cry, we seek, we peek,
But never delve, or dwell upon problems and time.
Could all things be re-written now and then?
Better get on and don't be long.
Otherwise time would unwind and go faster,
Till there's a deadly ominous zone.

What Is It About Love?

Oh tell the truth about love,
Love is like a weird but soulful food, or an aphrodisiac.
Love is quality, creative, mesmerising it's like a divine quest,
Thy love is powerful, loss, to think of now,
Than the sorrow of a sea of souls,
But thy breath, a zest of heaven scent, wise and wisdom.
Love is strange, it's like pebbles and sand, needs its charm,
Charisma, bouncing back from the goodness or a rift in time,
Needs its eternity or hole black,
Like peaches and cream, go soothing for a dessert,
And strawberries and cream are a goddesses dream.

That's Entertainment

The Writer
Writer required,
Paper, or typewriter, or computer,
A room required,
Photographs and memorabilia,
But no pen.

The Actors
A theatre, stage room required,
Actors, actresses enquired,
Sound effects on the double,
Oh no! Theres trouble!
Mustn't grumble,
No producer,
No director.

The Musicians
A room, hall, available,
Song sheets, verses, available,
The public to their seats,
Singers, performers, confused.
Oh no, not again, no conductor!

The Comedians
Audience waiting and stately, patiently,
Musicians ready,
The theatre ready,
Comedy writers, guest stars ready,
No not again,
No comedian!

Ode To Marie

Oh Marie's bright, sweet, so light, alls fair beauty,
Your smiles are wonderful, beautiful. Elegant lady.
Such a shimmering sight oh Marie.
You're lovely, flowing with magic,
Your voice is like a melancholy sound like making music,
You evaporate the fear, the darkness
But surround it with a glittering, fab, creative energy.
An Ode to Marie, a glossy, shiny lively soul,
So remarkable, shiny essence, you're better than money,
Better than sugar, sweets, you're a delightful honey.

Who Is That Girl?

Who's that girl, what girl?

Was she "the one"? She was bubbly, lively like a song,

A cheerful girl with beauty across her face,

Lovely, bright, breezy, never loses the smile from a trace.

When a cry or a tear dropped, evaporate from your shiny face.

Who was she?

It's a girl with the gold necklace,

Sparkling over there, with a heart shaped, around,

Lovely lass, so calm pure, beauty so sound.

When we weren't a match it was a shame

But always remained friends we depended on,

Remember love, you're the mysterious girl,

Wonderful terrific, fun loving, wicked sense of humour.

As were friends to me, you're still the girl that melted my heart.

Though we see each other as friends, we're not apart.

You're the girl, and still are.

Her name is Kate. A fantastic mate.

Who Am I?

Who am I?
I am the Doctor.
No, a doctor of all things.
Not a doctor but a timelord, no less, from Gallifrey
Sounds like a distant cloud or a planet of a burning sun
Where timelords live, both bad and good
Or even on the run.

Who am I?
I am the doctor.
No, a doctor of all things,
Not a doctor, but yes, THE Doctor!
The Doctor number one, stole a type 40 TARDIS
From his own race fifty years ago.
And a BBC sci-fi show was born.

Who am I?
I am a doctor.
Doctor who of course, I am the Doctor.
A timelord, ahh, timeless.
An alien humanoid that shares adventures in time and space
Here, there and everywhere.
Rocking through planets and defeating enemies,
Laughing through fear.
No tears, plenty of magical spheres.
Psychedelic music, so eerie,
Beneath or behind the sofa
Where memories are a reflection of trust.
The doctor.

Who am I?

I am the Doctor

Yes, the Doctor, not a doctor,

But the Doctor, how's he gonna get out of this one?

Will he be toast, or can he save the day?

There's been many faces,

So many companions.

Some have married or wanted to help on future planets.

A few sadly have died.

Who am I?

I am the Doctor.

But yes, I am definitely the Doctor, that's me.

To My Valentine

To my Valentine,
If you're a dancer,
Would you be a dancing partner?
I'd do a dance just for you,
Shall we dance, to take a chance and trance?
That's why you could be my romantic valentine.

If I was a singer,
I'd be a crooner,
Or just a jazz singer,
Possibly, yeah, a rock 'n' roll swinger,
I'd write a song for you, oh yes it's true,
You my dear, would be an ideal valentine,
Everyone's a winner, though not a deadly sinner.

Ohhh, if I was your comedian,
I would guarantee you lots of laughs,
But no put offs, all the jokes,
Cool, clean ones of course.
So babes, when you're feeling low or emotional,
I'd be sure a hit.
Make your funny bone tickle,
Be that valentine to wine and dine.

If I was your artist,

I'd paint a romantic picture,

Full of grace, beauty, and what a mixture.

Want to sketch you, oh yes it's time,

As a self portrait and sell it to the modern Tate.

That's why I want to be your valentine.

From the heart, so please be my valentine,

Would you be my valentine,

So we could both dine?

Definitely let us both entwine

With songs, soul and plenty of wine.

A Question Of Time

If time ran out, the world's end finished,
Capoosh, caput, what then?
Well i think we'd evaporate in thin air,
Vanish, gone in a second, or two.
That would make us all feel low and blue,
Best thing to do is take time as a friend,
It's so precious on this strange, outland, weird, smooth world,
Keep all your things stuck with us and cherish every moment we've got.
Because, one day, one world, time will stop and seize,
In standard animation, shocking but weary, but could be true.
As an englishman on this world, enjoy the karma of life
With fun, no worries and hell no strife,
But with laughter, humour, poetry, tea and cakes,
Beers, women, wine and song,
Love, happiness, where we all belong.

Take A Chill Pill

Relax, wine and dine is the thing.

Unwind is fine,

Cool, confident.

Relax like art,

A fine piece of taking it easy and as poetry to A.B.C speakeasy.

Plenty of tea. Cups of tea.

Feel better to unwind, and feel at ease calm, very relaxed, soothing,

Not in pain, not in any strain, nor going insane.

Plenty of Doctor Who to watch, and books of Doctor Who to read

That send myself into a happy dimension or another time, another world!

And get back home for tea.

One other thing though…

Art is groovy, fab, fun, smart, cool,

Outstanding, fine, and precious, amazing.

That's before bed, after a long mad day being like a zoomy busy bee.

A French Love

Travelling through romantic scenery of elegant Paris,
Twas I walked down the town and the street,
To meet and greet, have a coffee, cafe,
Then down to the river Seine,
Then up the Eiffel tower, to the art gallery.
Where alas I saw the most enigmatic tall and attractive
But mysterious shiny personality.
A smile.

So refreshing and a lust of life, hell no strife,
I felt I wanted to mingle, though I'm single,
But crikey, my heart was gleaming and twinging,
A Paris love, brunette, with the most enthralling smile that glistened,
My heartbeat felt twist 'n' soothe, wow what an amazing lady
Of emerald green eyes, in a mellow yellow dress.
But she knew who I was,
"Madellinea."
She sighed.
"Shaine."
I cried.
It was fifteen years since we last met, our hearts were set on fire,
All our passions thrived upon us again with desires,
But aww f*ck! No, oh poo!
Married.

What a weird, strange french brief encounter,
Never mind, I was fifteen years miles too late,
Never mind, on so far,
Maybe it was a mistake,
Destiny or even serendipity of fate.

Africa, War, Peace

Oh what on earth is war?
Blooming wrong 'uns, doings, killings,
Like a shattered dismal scar.
War is like a beast, deadly like a poisonous snake,
War is displeasing, not nice, a hefty price to cost,
As lives are shattered and lost.

Peace, we need to unite as one,
Understanding is better to resolve,
Like a hummingbird song,
It's all political, fight for rights,
But don't use force or neglect but respect.
The third worlds, with issues of sickness, and Aids.
If someone is ill, think before you have more children,
Jobs are hard to get searching.
Crikey, Africa is a whole centrepoint of planters
And pasts so big, so hot, in the tropical jungle.
Wildbush tea is nice,
Its elegant flavour is fragrantly strong,
Like a herby fennel seed or stalk.

Dancing And Clubbing

Clubbing, it's as cool as ice, mint, exciting,
Fun and amazing, its anticipating.
Which flows adrenaline rush.
The dances you have now, so sexy to mention,
Like music lovers in heaven, or boom boom to the beat of the drums,
Where starry eyed lovers, heartbeat being a pace to any place
Or euphoria or somewhere parallel.

Clubbing. Have a cocktail or two,
Dancing till the early hours that's true.
A place to dance, have a jolly wicked time,
A way to dance into trance, techno, flava, reggae, samba.
So naughty, raunchy, or a place to flirt.
Is there any room to wine and dine or eat?
Book to have a private party hire,
Maybe have the song played "Girl on Fire".

Dancers are getting very saucy,
Makes your heart go ping, or it makes you sing.
Music is the power of love, it's a dove.
Dating is another thing, it's magic, creative love,
So let's get connected, find a date or a soul mate,
Flirt, it's like thirst, adrenaline lies and in the rushes.

The sight of people you know, dancing,
Body to body, hip to hip, or passionately.
Dancers giving out enigma signs of flirt, or 'I like you'.
Eye contact is the great healer and spark, lets connect.

Dancing, clubbing is like a film.
It's sweet smell of success, for princesses and princes.
As it's all beauty, all wise, all wonderful.
Beautiful.

A Day In The Life Of

Once upon a time,
150 or 160 years ago,
A horrible sad thing happened,
A place called institutions.
What a blow, oh no!
Some people liked it, some people loathed it,
Some suffered in silence,
Or made them never speak again.
Terrible, but thousands of years of disability rights,
Were never allowed to have a voice,
Were never thought of.
We were treated like freaks, with beaks,
Like the greatest freak show in the Galaxy.
Put into institutions, or blocks,
Did the people in there care, or really give a damn,
In that dreadful Victorian era?
So where are we now?
Yes, we overcame the tears.
We overcame the fears.
Did we want to do the Great Escape?
Of course we bloomin' wanted to!
Why is society so happy, so happy with how we look?
Goodness knows.
It's all getting slightly better,
Hopefully forever.
We all can live as one,
On this mad, shattering, crazy weather world.
Come on Earth!
No more destruction, cleansing minority.
No Death.
Peace and love from an angel above.

Rumble In The Jungle

Twas down south, a beautiful red sunset,
There lived a snake called Percy, who liked to party,
And a crocodile called Darcy,
With a carnivorous, smug grin,
Who liked a bit of gin,
He took a disliking to Roderick, the clumsy Ant Aardvark.
Darcy said "I don't like you because your snout
Left some of your ants in my snappy toned teeth."

Cradox the Hyena laughed himself to sleep.
But swallowed a bug and went beep with hiccups.

Bettie the african grey parrot was wise and gentle,
Loved humans, and they loved her.
But Bettie the parrot rejoiced her love of carrots, nuts and fruits.

Bean the baboon loved comedy and thought
He's a loon, so went into cartoons.
The bongo, mango, the bango loved to play the double bass
And play with an all animal ball orchestra.

Zora the Zebra was adventurous, charm and full of calm
And helped perform in the zoo and have tea too.

Dastan the blue monkey, was very naughty
And packed up his troubles to perform
In a rumble in the jungle choir.
Any conductors for hire???

All Things Light

Light, what on earth is it?

Who invented it?

Is light the key to the darkness or fairest?

It's all things light so bright, a latin night,

Its a bulb of scientific discovery,

Electrifying sound of a shimmering sight.

Light is absorbing delight from darkness,

Brings out mysterious dark skies, cloudy nights.

Light brings peace, harmony tranquility,

Energy of a smile with warmth on a fair maiden's face,

That gives you funny particles, that twists and soothes one heart,

Like it melts butter, light is the colour yellow.

This creative spectacle is magic though mellow and entwining melancholy.

The people of this world, what do you think light is?

Strange things without a light or lamp,

You'd have problems so severe, or bump into household items,

With sharp crashing bangs!

The shade and the thump, the mortified drums of a thunder storm!

Well if no light so bright standing tall to give the towns safe at night,

The world will be with darkness

Into shades of Victorian or Edwardian England.

So dark and despair with no happiness,

Dignity but a dark, moody, broody, city.

With life so down in a state of depression.

So light is a powerful, wise, truly beautiful everyday usage,

We have, it's our enlightenment, our entertainment.

Beauty

What is beauty?
Is it the personality?
Love, and looks is a dark catastrophe,
What counts? Is it looks?
They say what lies in the eye of the beholder,
Is it ugly, when someone looks at you and "EEK".
"No good god, get away! You're definitely not my type! NO thank you!!!"

That has happened to me thousands of times,
Well we are all human, give us respect.
Not nice suddenly looking into a mirror and looking kind of hairy,
And overgrown furry ears.
No, haha! Only joking, not me!

But rejection of love or being asked to dance
Is a fear of attraction or beauty.
But when you look into someones eyes, wahey!
You know that there's instant chemistry and not full blown history.
That is when beauty is in the eye of the beholder,
Love doesn't have to "Look at me, aren't I gorgeous" looks,
Personally i'd always rather go for personality.

Clara Oswin

As Easter is fast morphing, a televison legend is back
Doctor Who hits our screens, yay, with a 50th anniversary 1963-2013.

But one thing matters of time and space is Oswin or Clara Owsin.
Who is she? We've seen her twice before, died suddenly,
Was a dalek as Oswin, Oswin (Clara) Oswald, nanny barmaid died then.
But let's hope the doctor can save this one.
Their dynamic, creative, sparkly.
Their partnership is like a dance or vision of beauty.
Like a double act of Hepburn and Tracy.

Can't wait, it's an adrenaline rush,
Urban thriller. Not a mind dweller, or, ohh, aww, I...oh gosh!

Clara is now a modern day, lovely lady.
But who on earth will she be?
The impossible girl.
Well the doctor's been searching the universe
To find out who, when, why and her.
Monsters of old and new, creatures, aliens, Daleks to scare and shock.
Oh the thrills, the spills in beans, been too blumin' windy!
See inside the Tardis, wowzers, awesome, cool ship of time.
Wish I had one, never mind. One day I shall come back.

Will there be a fifth dimension?
There has already been a fourth dimension, a world in creation
Chemistry to see how the Doctor dances with Clara.
Is it parralell, a destiny, a date, a fate, or serendipity.
So Doctor who fans young and old, keep you eyes peeled.
All will be revealed.

Old Time Paris & Now

I went to an art gallery, in London,
As I looked with passion and beauty,
Vibrant colours, a dash of fresh light, a bright sight to see,
What life was in fact like, a society.
And after that i came across the amazing spectacle of a painting of
France I was in awe of, so whimsical, fabulous, colourful zest,
Brash of humour, or a romantic scenery, attractive, so sweet,
Like a magical idea of try and do art, from the heart.

But after the pleasing day, times passed,
Swiftly like an in-tune vision.
Maybe I was sleeping, is this an illusion?
Is it in high definition?
Am I hallucinating?
Or in blurred vision or images?

Aww, bother, im in the painting of that very fine piece of art.
A groovy rift in time possibly, caressing the part of art.
Seeing what other artists did,
Obviously went and drank too much, betted too much.
And the can-can, a musical and laughter, artists, poets,
Wonder if Van Gogh went there, alas care 'twas fair,
See the Eiffel tower, built in 1889.
Come and have a coffee, but I realised to go home
Before someone had a panic attack.

Ladies and gents, do not adjust your paintings.
I fell into a trance in France.

Eternals

What is an eternal? Hmm, "A fascinating race",
Ghost like creatures of beauty.
In their times pace, but they really are creepy and tragic,
Maybe light, magic is in equal measure,
Could they be finding treasure?
Do they have fortunes, features or any desires?
Their place in the universe is scattered about
As an emptiness of infinite existence,
As echoes of darkness or light, no pact,
No care in the world, or something or someone.
But one thing they may know is, they may find out what love is!
Think it's a sparkle or a tear from ones eye,
Be careful what you ask for, or even wish for, it might not be cool.
You'd be a threat, or even thwarted, or just,
Aww roast toast, so be it being a sad fool.
Enlightenment is wisdom to your hearts desire,
But lives might turn into powder or fire,
So don't choose immortality or eternal youth,
New life, or enlightenment. Choose love, choose life.

If Love Was Another Dimension

If love was exciting, what would it be if there was a parallel universe?
Would it be the same or will there be a lot of hell to blame?
What is love?! They usually say it's two dimensional but is it though?
I ask you....
Is it a crime, a rhyme, a journey, bliss, happiness?
Nobody knows.
Deja vu.
Do you get that most of the time?
It's a funky sign, dangerous or weird timeline,
Love is the good cause,
I'd like to find out the meaning of love, again,
Instead of being in a strain or hurts in pain.

Illusions

What is an illusion? Well, they're a trick or something quick,
Something like a quick discovery of someone
Or something that's not there before,
Like the saying goes, "Before your eyes",
Is it powerful, or strange like an adventure of someday,
Somewhat estranged?
Is illusions science and magic or fatal and tragic?
Can it be fearful, lost in standard animation
Or a near scientific creation, or ambition?
Daredevil magicians, like Harry Houdini, the master of escapology.
But was he crackers, or isolated though.
Some of his illusion acts were terrifying,
Death defying like David Blaine.
Is he from another planet, or just too clever for acts as sinister pacts.
But what we see is graceful, wise, like a jedi mind trick.
Illusions are out of this world, or the unknown,
Or magnificent spectacular, images of what we see is just creepy,
Mesmerising, mind blowing or just outstanding.
Or the ITV2's Ben Hainlen of "Tricked", wow, authentic,
Fresh and thrilling for a received audience.
Dynamo, mad as a warlock or insane wizard of Lord Valdemot of
Harry Potter or Stephen Mulhern, a great magician and TV presenter.
And a timelord's trick is regeneration, cheating death,
And hope it's body repaired, cell by cell
With this almagest of particles of light beams,
And surrounds the old body and reinvents the new,

Then these new doctors have quirkiness,

Eccentricity or something crazy, dark for a new dimension.

That's the story of magic.

Illusions are awesome in every way, mind boggling.

Never keep your eyes off the performer, intriguing as it seems.

Never blink.

Your mind, soul, might sink.

Millennium 1999 And Beyond

We are the human race.

What will we all be like in a few years or years pace?

Will there be aliens roaming the universe or the place?

Kappa shoes that tingle with electric light or glow in the dark.

Or bouncy shoes, like moon boots,

Like you're walking on the moon or any strange atmosphere.

Will TV exist still or change into digital HD films,

Still continue to blosson through the ages.

Is there lifeforces or telekinetic forces in the atmosphere,

Come on see and share?

Will cars fly or glide through the air?

Maybe better than the price of petrol, diesel or fuels.

Youngsters come and see their world as a nation for all of life's creations.

Is it moon boots and dinner suits

And have dinner at the end of the universe.

Are there computer viruses or a not so jolly good curse?

I think it will be ok, not sure about computers,

Oh, they crash and burn and go warp-drive.

Facebook, Youtube, Twitter and all the magical images

Of bebo and snapchat or instagram.

Where the hell did time go? It's a crime, blimey it's 2014!

We had the Olympics, 450 years since the birth of William Shakespeare,

Author, art thou a song for space and fears or sharp spheres,

The bi-centenery of the birth of Charles Dickens.

Dylan Thomas (Poet), both brilliant fab writers, poets, storytellers.

But wow, what next?

Flying bikes, pouring taps of lemonade or herbal tea,

HD TVs, magical kettles for pots of teas.

Invisible cars, that go oh so far.

Holograms of instructions, or in theatre space dust of time travel.

Will we see the stars, milky way, planets of two suns,

Other dimensions of sounds of reality.

What about teleportation....I wonder hmmm.

Will it be starting to travel in style,

Go through worlds places in any other radius of miles.

I know you all might be thinking,

He's been watching too much Doctor Who!

The truth is, what out there? Nobody knows.

The Girl With The Green Eyes

Girl with a heart, like a lovely lady with elegance and grace

You make my heart beat to 100%,

Oh dear sweet beauty of green eyes,

Could I go for a date?

Wow with a smile like that, would reach me everyday just before tea.

Babe it's you i'd like to get to know, you see a passionate,

Wow so bubbly, kind, outgoing,

Get to know you first, otherwise if we didn't it all gets worse,

Or perhaps even a curse.

Don't like it when it goes wrong, makes everything get bad, mad, sad,

What we need is a jolly good time together,

The girl who stole my heart away and melted it away like butter,

That butter flutter and made me me stutter, dear sweet Kelly.

You're beautiful, kind, sweet natured, friendly, soul songbird,

I liked you from the start but found it hard,

As you didn't want to be filmed.

What Is It About Love?

Oh tell me the truth about love.

Love is like a weird but soulful food,

Or an aphrodisiac. Love is quality, creative,

Mesmerising though love's a divine quest.

Thy is powerful loss, as it's to think of now,

Then the sorrow, or of a sea of souls,

But thee breath, zest of heaven scent, wise and wisdom.

Love is magical, serious, mental, to cool for sure, manic, witty, arty,

The sound of love, of all things beautiful, like sand 'n' pebbles,

That needs to embrace its shell and pace,

Loved with a pattery shade of charisma,

Bouncing back from the goodness,

Or possibly if a rift in time needs it's eternity,

Or hole black loves wish is too entwined,

Or food of light peaches and cream are soothing for a dessert,

And strawberries and cream a heavenly goddesses dream.

But love is good, it's not made of wood,

It's a masterpiece of wit, joy and emotion, its pure absolution.

Such a thing called love is the smooth, lost soul quest,

Find it before we rest.

A, B, C, D

You're so funny, A said to B,

You're so vain said B to A,

Haha cried C, you're both daft, I'm much better than you,

I'm pointy and politer than you, replied C,

But D thought, damn cheek to C, think you're Mr know-it-all.

About Me, I

I am Shaine, a poet, actor and sometimes a writer.

Mostly my life has been in disasters. A student of many talents.

Always happy to be here, wherever and whatever the weather.

Among faces of old and new.

But always crack a smile, you know? Never know how to stop.

I like to make afternoon tea delights, don't need to eat a lot, could pop!

A Doctor Who fan by trade,

It's been a fairly hard old life I've made.

Honey

Honey, so runny and sweet and funny,

Sandwiches are so yummy.

Gorgeous, sweet nectar of busy buzzy bees,

A journey oh so far.

Find out when honey was established or happily started,

But why did your mum have my honey sandwiches?

But really what's happening to our bees and the population?

It's possibly chemicals or something else.

Not nice to be precise,

That's why honey, is my honey bunny.

Head Over Heels

Head over heels, I'm head over heels in love,
You're the sweetest, loveliest dove.
Was lost, then broken before, now love has blossomed for some,
It feels what the world needs is love.
It's about time too, as the Beatles say in their songs,
Love is all you need.

Let everyone know, let's all get head over heels in love,
Only if you want to though, not lost in translation,
But a loving anticipation, love action, not a love distraction,
Love pouring in or out, not apart, or about,
No persuasion,
But confidence, as love is quite peculiar, strong,
Weird or weary, but never make love go wrong.

I'm head over heels in love,
Please, my dear, be the dove,
Before our hearts leapt time broken,
Want it go steady, fun, free, wise - not go rotten.
Definitely not lost into rock bottom.

Summer Of Love

Summer of love, it feels sweet, like honey,

Calm, and happy days, it's kinda funny.

In a way, it feels like we transported back to 1967, the summer of love.

Peace dedicated followers of fashion,

Smartly, toe tapping, dance, like in a haze.

But don't take any pills or anything, but seize the day and enjoy.

All that free love, where did it all go?

But in the times now, we have get-togethers, beaches, BBQ's, art festivals,

Beer festivals, poetry in motion, music festivals, Edinburgh fringe,

And Somerset House film festival, or any guided tour.

'Twas Before Christmas

A cold brisk winter, so white sky like ice cream, or marshmallows,
Like a pure delight, a wonderous sight,
Christmassy, bright, cheerful light.
It's like a pale silver shadow, inches of white snow,
Surrounding areas a blow.
Carol singing, nativities so brilliant, poignant Christmas songs
Heard on the radio, HD TV, or stereo.
Plays of a Christmas Carol, of ghosts of past, present, future,
Or of what's to come.
And thrills, spills, splendid chills,
Pantomimes, for timeless timelines.
A wishful Merry Christmas to you all.
Be the belle of the ball!

Christmas Is Coming

December has fallen, like a warm scented snow,
As November is now a distant shadow.
With bleak winters night so cold,
Not as bright but a wintery crisp delight.
Keep cool, and warm, calm and full of charm
As Christmas is coming, strangely as it seems,
It's zooming like fast timeways, like a journey of days.

December is now in the mist of time,
January silently storming through, like an echo or whisper,
And only then will December's ghost be time.

Pantomimes, plays, "A Christmas Carol",
By the superb, awesome writer Charles Dickens.
If he was still alive, I'd love to work alongside an author,
Possibly to meet a brilliant creator of plays, or a modern day writer.
Christmas is coming, who, what, when?
A Christmas miracle, or an oracle, like something magical.
As each day looms and shines,
Decembers life cycle is a morphing light shrine.

About Time

About time, is it divine, is it a thread?

Unique or a timeline, particles of a harmonious zone?

Is time a clone or a drone? Can time be a loan?

Ah yes, possibly spare moments of reality, of borrowed time.

It's a discovery, can we one day go back in time for the right reason,

Love to all seasons.

Go back to Victorian, but more Edwardian era,

To see what life was like in Bournemouth's Miramar.

Still the loveliest hotel I've seen, it's still my favourite place,

Still in a poet, or winter's dream.

So about time, can it be rewritten,

Or will it be a re-energised poignant version

As we change the things we do for the better.

Let time not be the ole devil moon,

But lead the powerful divine thread of reality itself.

In and out of time but through,

Let love be the one of all times passions.

Love, Is It A Collector's Item?

Love is strange, does it like change?

It's bonkers, I tell ya,

It's fascinating, crackers.

Is it a poem of old and new? Though could it be a collectors item

Or a special edition or an easter egg feature on a DVD?

Love has it's narrow moments,

Are they magic, are they tragic?

It's creative, a creation of scientific particles of light, lost visions of souls

Like fluttery butterflies that make us or break us.

The true glory of love, I tell you,

Is time passion, truth, commitment, wine, dine, funky rhymes.

Most important of all trust - before love turns into crust

Or scattered toast or dust.

Particles Of Christmas Cheer

All things Christmas, dark nights,

December sights, wholesome delights,

Cold snap wintery days gives us a chill, spell,

Of all happy particles of Christmas cheer,

Awesome scent of winters spice with all things cinnamon and nice,

Particles of Christmas spread the joy and cheer, plenty of magical tears,

Joy, peace, laughter, humour, with bursts of yellow,

Or happy orange energy of light,

A delicate particle so bright,

Light of multi-coloured Christmas tree lights,

That twinkle in the air, or in the skies fair.

Identity

Everyone has an identity, or DNA,
A source of biology, strange science and technology.
Creative and pure bliss, respect and dignity.
A timelord has the DNA of Gallifrey,
900 or 1200 now, the world, cool man,
A lord of time, with a ship of time called the TARDIS,
With two hearts, if one stops beating or pounding,
It's a near death experience for us humans. It's the end.
Wouldn't mind having two hearts.
But I'm cool just having one, it would be very weird,
But the DNA of my identity is poetry,
It's classical, funny, a good old fashioned romp with plenty of humour,
Some drama or sad trauma, but i'm best remembered for love poetry.
I'm polite, cool, quirky, all teeth and curls, sometimes great on fashion.
Art and poetry and me, is the perfect identity.

Cancer

What is it?

It's horrible, terrible, fearful, tragic.

Damn well not fair, we struggle to share, and care,

Is it a black hole?

We fall in and get sucked in from the atmosphere.

Haven't a clue.

Is it a weasel?

Nobody knows.

It spots, lumps, bumps,

Just want to stamp on,

People going through it,

Is a terrible time.

Is there a sign?

There is, there is hope through a traumatic journey,

Just check yourself regularly.

Hopefully we can save quite a few more people,

It's worth helping others,

Work together, stamp down those fears and tears, emotions.

No pain, no gain,

All have a great recovery,

And a holiday in Spain.

Best of luck to those going through it.

Easter Time

When all things come and spring into action.

A bud grows from seed, to everlasting love and joy of aromas,

Scent of flowers, everything in bloom.

As a nation we come together, poetry in motion,

To celebrate the meaning of Easter,

Feast on or have a siesta.

Birds tweeting, little chicks are chirpy chirpy cheeek,

Saying eeek, eeek, tweet.

With tiny feathers, chirping, eeky beak or squeak.

But alas, here comes chocolate, easter egg hunts for – AHA!

A chocolate treasure laid for lunch, supper or even for pleasure.

Easter bunnies, chocolate.

By the way, bunny rabbits are not just for Easter.

Great as pets, with all the carrots you can think,

Gosh, that's a lot of carrot juice, freshly squeezed, with a hint of lemon.

The true meaning of Easter time, palm Sunday and before that lent.

Goody Friday, such a joy.

Hot cross buns with lovely tea and butter.

Lovely jubbly.

Animal

There is a cat inside me that is always tired,
But the busy sleepy cat, should have retired.

There is a bull that inside me plays rugby, but when he played the game,
He destroyed the ball with his sharp, spiky horns.
So that's why he never ever played rugby.
So he took up dodgeball, which he always loved,
He said it was better than rugby.

There in me is a mouse who is a detective mouse,
Who seems to browse, cos he's always on the case.
Also always after the villains that's why he's the best detective in a million.
When he saves the day or night, someone is going to be killed.
He could even save the world.

At The Circus

The Circus,
With tension grows upon the stage,
Adrenaline flows with uproarious rage.
The hustle and bustle from the audience grows,
How many out there? Nobody knows.
The Harness, built for circus and plays, in mid air,
But if you're not used to heights, oh what a fright.
Otherwise you may be in dizzy heights
Though if you're an adrenaline junkie,
Then it would be oh so funky.
Dancers of the trapeze,
Do you think, when you watch, are they a tease?
Seriously though, when you look at them carefully,
You may freeze at ease.
See dancers glide, fly and pirouette,
Like loves of Romeo and Juliet,
Or maybe Rod and Bet.
Up and up and up, away they go.
Wow, higher and higher, rocketing to the moon.
(Do they want to come down too soon?)
On one thing, be careful of the villainous Deldrum,
Half man, all stone or rubble,
But be careful, that Deldrum faces his enemy or his victims,
Doesn't turn on you, you'd be in a heap of trouble.

Or Medusa, are they friends or fiends?
Jugglers juggle balls, as many as they can,
Or spinning top plates, would be fun with your mates.
Singers, actors, dancers, clowns,
Musicians, performers, collaborate together.
In the worlds exciting years,
With no fear,
We can do this,
Be an historical event,
Nobody's ever going to forget.

Bus Stop

I'm waiting for a bus
One hot Easter Sunday
Off to mum's for lunch
Just after mid-day

I look on up
At the busy road ahead
Minding my own business
A poem in my head.

Suddenly from the left
A big black jeep appears
Window winds down, blasting
House music and jeers.

Then it speeds off
Round the Wessex Way
And comes back again
Now what'll they say?

I recognise one of them
From Youth Service shows
I used to read poems
He used to break dance.

Now here we both are
On Easter Sunday
A voice in my head says
HELP!

I sat there a long time
Lost and alone
Stuck forever
In the Danger Zone.

Why did he turn on me?
He used to be friendly.
My life's all gone wrong
I'm eaten up with envy.

He showed me up
In front of his mates!
He's such a cool dude
And I'm just a loser.

So that's it for me
Something has died.
I've lost an old friend -
No more poetry.

Help Me

Help me I'm being bullied,
I feel tortured and abandoned
I feel physically sick, drained,
Am I that loser?
Although you feel I'm not
But sadly, I do feel that I am.

Who and when or why do they pick on me?
So they say, they think it's funny,
But I damn feel hurt and numb,
Or maybe suicidal at times.

I feel better now, feeling even better and better
As I shall go on, let it flow
And let my love, as life gets good,
Let it show.

Autumn

Autumn is an atmospheric, misty month.
The weather that I love.
Leaves float in mid-air, windy-bright and breezy,
Multi-coloured leaves are great to find. It's so easy.
The dampened weather make me feel dazey.

I have a passion for writing poetry and drama,
So I don't become lazy.
Leaves are oh so colourful,
The air looks so beautiful,
The distance of space and the atmosphere in the air
Is scented and is so magical.

Acorns falling from the oak trees, dancing in the morning mist
Gathered in the squirrel's fists.
Though these multi-coloured leaves drift down
Laying a carpet of copper, russet and gold
Covering conkers of shining brown.

Wind is passing by, don't know why.
The wind is like friend you can depend, but it sees eye to I,
As I stood wondering on an Autumn day,
Looking up at the moon passing by,
Into the next day,
Through the forest I stay.

A Penny For The Guy

Guy Fawkes, he sits on top of the bonfire
Waiting for his dreadful fate.
The flames are beginning to flicker,
Warming us all as the hour is late.
As we stand and sip our steaming soup
Cheesy hot jacket potatoes fresh from the warm fire,
Juicy, succulent hot dogs with taste buds of all one's desires.

Roasting chestnuts from the warm fire for all our group.
Colourful Catherine wheels go whizzzzzzzzzz,
Round and round.
Glittery sparkles, write our own names in the dark air,
Silver and gold fountains flow to the ground.
Rockets shoot up into the sky as we stand and stare.

The Book of
Shaine

Love & Romance

Love and romance, what a way to go,
From finding love or to losing love,
But sex is a scary bit, every time.
I know everyone does it, or not
But make sure you've both planned it
Before the time comes of day.

Otherwise, if no precautions, or pill,
Or a plan to start a life, then you're doomed.
Plus that will be too bad.
Losing love is also sad, bad and very hard.
So make love and sex, romance.
A wonderful time planning it.
Before it's too late.

Karen Gillan

A flame haired red head of pure mystery did move,
A former model turned actress.
A Scottish beauty of the small screen and now the big screen.
Full of praise, sunshine, poise, smooth,
Like an artist's or poets dream, or a muses art scene,
Like clear honey of golden nectar, sweet shimmering bird of desire.
Actress played Amy Pond, or "Amelia",
Wise cracker, soul-diva, flame haired, feisty and fancy free.

Creature of beauty, wisdom.
As a Scottish myth or mystery siren of innocence.
A zest for life, a bright star, she'll do well.
As far as a magic show, she has a flair for stylish fashion
Versatile belle of the ball. Oh, she's wild as an orchid or herb.
Joyful bright spirit, excellent, wise, full of sunshine, hope,
A breath of fresh air, now an actress in America.

A charming, cool collective, creative spectacle of a bubbly personality.
Wow, thy ist a Scottish rose,
So brimming with cheers and shiny happy jeers.

Love Has Its Goods & Bads

Love has it's goods and bads,
Sometimes good, and the bads – don't be sad.
Remember the fun times together,
Forget the tough times too.
If you ever feel blue, try out other ideas, true.

So that's time to stick together, forever
Or to make up or break up.

Never Let Go

Never let go.
I will never forget my time with you.
Sometimes I begin to wonder why you went and left me,
Why did you go?

My life has gone on long and low
From the earth, universe, space you did go.
I've tried to move on,
But I hate it when my life goes wrong.

I feel lost, in translation, love is a total distraction.
What a way to go.
I forgive you, but I bloody well miss you.
Always.

I wish I could have had a better say
There could have been another way.

Goodbye for now my lovely sweet pea
Wish we could have had more time (possibly for tea).
But never mind, that's life
And love for us, you see.

Hate Crime

Hate crime, is a deadly enemy,
They say it can be your friend
If it is, then it's called a frenemy.
It's evil, sadistic,
Not charming nor charismatic.
Stamp down those tears, those fears,
The gritty side, the dark side,
Times are a changing.
Respect, live to a prospect.
Join the Mencap.
Take action.
Spread the word.
End the silence
As crime can not be rewritten.
End disability hate crime.
There will be a time.

Scars Of War

Tension grows upon the trenches, not divine, not nice
Pain, fear, death, loss, friend or foe.
As scars of war, disgusting to see, bleak, not perfect
Not wise, of lives gone in a second, or a flash
A hefty cost of ones life, to be precise.
It's like a game of chess, a dice with decision making
Or death, no health.

Tension grows upon the trenches,
Not like a holiday or a breakaway, fear
Life now is called stress disorder, or something like it.
The bodies surround the holes of the trenches,
Shards of ammunition, glass or dust all over them.
Sad loss of those who never come back.
Sadly shocking truth struck, no happiness, but no joy or luck.

As tension goes and flows up the nowhere,
Dusts of clouds where the trenches' fallen heroes fall
And be remembered ever more, now 100 years on, lest we forget
Those loyal and faithful heroes that never came back.

The Goffink Monster

He's a life threatening disaster,
Full of razor sharp brown teeth,
Spotty black and purple skin.
Warning – don't approach him!
Beware the Goffink monster!

With his blood shot eyes,
He's contageous, outrageous,
Always on the look out for
Fresh victims, fresh blood!
Beware the Goffink monster!

Cruel, vicious, cunning, hard,
Big as a mountain,
Hot as a volcano,
He's coming to get you!
Beware the Goffink monster!

He'll gobble you up,
He'll rip you to shreds,
He's a living nightmare.
He'll make you wet the bed!
(You could wake up dead).
Beware the Goffink monster!

continued...

Maybe it's revenge,
Maybe he's just unkind,
Maybe it's because
Of his spotty behind!
Beware the Goffink monster!

Us lot all live in fear!
We tremble, we shake,
Can't sleep, lie awake.
Feel so useless, so small!
Because of the Goffink monster.

Why does he do it?
Is he out of control?
Or has he a master?
Can you reason with
The Goffink monster?

 The Book of Shaine

16452479R00038

Printed in Great Britain
by Amazon